HIS HOLY HOUSE

INSPIRATIONAL IMAGES
AND THOUGHTS ABOUT THE TEMPLE

Cover image: *Gate to Heaven—Manti Temple* © McNaughton Fine Art Co. Back cover image: *Salt Lake Temple at Night—Blue* © McNaughton Fine Art Co. For print information go to www.mcnaughtonart.com.
Cover and book design by Christina Ashby, © 2007 by Covenant Communications, Inc.

Published by Covenant Communications, Inc.,
American Fork, Utah

Printed in China
First Printing: September 2007

13 12 11 10 09 08 07   10 9 8 7 6 5 4 3 2 1

ISBN 978-1-59811-400-3

His Holy HOUSE

Manti Utah

This journey to higher ground is the pathway of discipleship to the Lord Jesus Christ. It is a journey that will ultimately lead us to exaltation with our families in the presence of the Father and the Son. Consequently, our journey to higher ground must include the house of the Lord. As we come unto Christ and journey to higher ground, we will desire to spend more time in His temples, because the temples represent higher ground, sacred ground.

Joseph B. Wirthlin, "Journey to Higher Ground," Ensign, Nov. 2005, 19

I have hallowed this house, which thou hast built, to put my name there for ever; and mine eyes and mine heart shall be there perpetually.

1 KINGS 9:3

Nauvoo Illinois

St. George Utah

he temple is concerned with things of immortality. It is a bridge between this life and the next. All of the ordinances that take place in the house of the Lord are expressions of our belief in the immortality of the human soul.

GORDON B. HINCKLEY, STAND A LITTLE TALLER [SALT LAKE CITY: DESERET BOOK, 2001], 6

Each temple building is an inspiration, magnificent and beautiful in every way, but the temple building alone does not bless. The endowed blessings and divine functions—involving much that is not of this world, such as priesthood keys—come through obedience and faithfulness to priesthood authority and covenants made.

JAMES E. FAUST, "'WHO SHALL ASCEND INTO THE HILL OF THE LORD?'"
ENSIGN, AUG. 2001, 2

Mount Timpanogos Utah

For behold, I have accepted this house, and my name shall be here; and I will manifest myself to my people in mercy in this house.

D&C 110:7

Albuquerque New Mexico

As a result of the sacred ordinances performed in the holy house of God, no light need be permanently extinguished, no voice permanently stilled, no place in our heart permanently left vacant.

THOMAS S. MONSON, BE YOUR BEST SELF [SALT LAKE CITY: DESERET BOOK, 1979], 54

Laie Hawaii

Sacramento California

The Latter-day Saints affirm that their vicarious work in behalf of the dead is required of them by the call of the Lord through direct revelation; and that it becomes the duty and privilege of every individual who accepts the Gospel and enters the Church to labor for the salvation of his dead. He is expected and required by the obligations and responsibility he has assumed as a member of the Church of Jesus Christ, so to live as to be a worthy representative of his departed ancestors, in holy ordinance, and to be of clean life, that he may not forfeit his right to enter the sacred confines of the Lord's House, where alone he may officiate in that privileged capacity.

JAMES E. TALMAGE, THE HOUSE OF THE LORD [SALT LAKE CITY: DESERET BOOK, 1968], 68

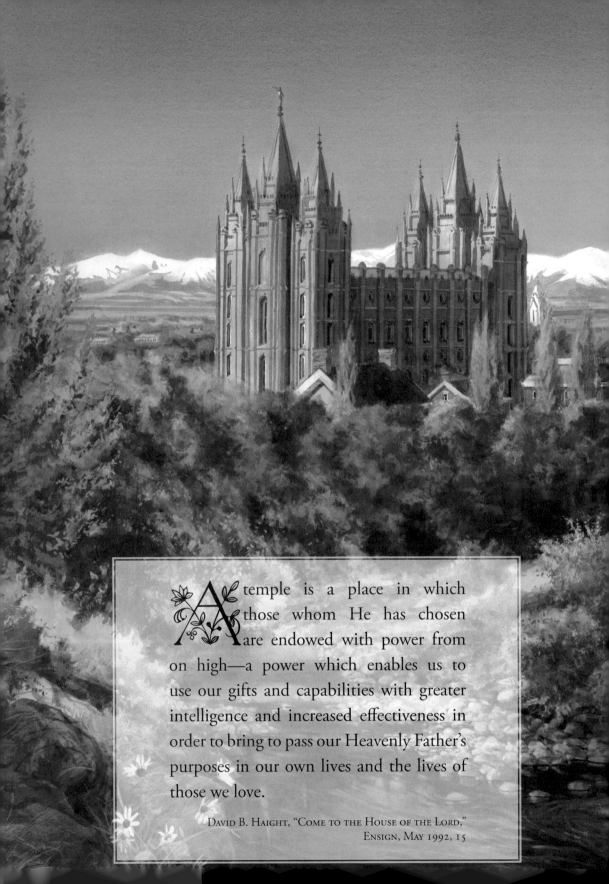

A temple is a place in which those whom He has chosen are endowed with power from on high—a power which enables us to use our gifts and capabilities with greater intelligence and increased effectiveness in order to bring to pass our Heavenly Father's purposes in our own lives and the lives of those we love.

David B. Haight, "Come to the House of the Lord," Ensign, May 1992, 15

Salt Lake City

Oakland California

I personally regard all of the houses of the Lord as the work of Jehovah, initiated by him, built by him, designed by him, and dedicated to him and his program.

SPENCER W. KIMBALL, FAITH PRECEDES THE MIRACLE [SALT LAKE CITY: DESERET BOOK, 1972], 32

What a glorious thing it is for us to have the privilege of going to the temple for our own blessings. Then after going to the temple for our own blessings, what a glorious privilege to do the work for those who have gone on before us. This aspect of temple work is an unselfish work. Yet whenever we do temple work for other people, there is a blessing that comes back to us. Thus it should be no surprise to us that the Lord does desire that his people be a temple-motivated people.

HOWARD W. HUNTER, "A TEMPLE-MOTIVATED PEOPLE,"
ENSIGN, FEB. 1995, 5

Seattle Washington

Buni Laura Wilson

San Diego California

The temple is the house of the Lord. The basis for every temple ordinance and covenant—the heart of the plan of salvation—is the Atonement of Jesus Christ. Every activity, every lesson, all we do in the Church, point to the Lord and His holy house. Our efforts to proclaim the gospel, perfect the Saints, and redeem the dead all lead to the temple. Each holy temple stands as a symbol of our membership in the Church, as a sign of our faith in life after death, and as a sacred step toward eternal glory for us and our families.

RUSSELL M. NELSON, "PERSONAL PREPARATION FOR TEMPLE BLESSINGS," ENSIGN, MAY 2001, 32

For behold, this is my work and my glory—to bring to pass the immortality and eternal life of man.

MOSES 1:39

Portland Oregon

Jordan River Utah

For verily this generation shall not all pass away until an house shall be built unto the Lord, and a cloud shall rest upon it, which cloud shall be even the glory of the Lord, which shall fill the house.

D&C 84:5

The temple is a place of holiness. It is the most sacred and holy place on earth and should be treated with the greatest degree of reverence and respect. Reverence in the temple is an expression to the Lord that we consider it to be sacred and that we recognize it to be, indeed, His holy house. . . . May we enhance our temple experience with a spirit of reverence, treating it as a place of purity and a place of holiness. . . . If we do these things, the Lord will bless us and we will become prepared to live in His holy presence.

L. Lionel Kendrick, "Enhancing Our Temple Experience," Ensign, May 2001, 78–79

St. George Utah

Salt Lake City

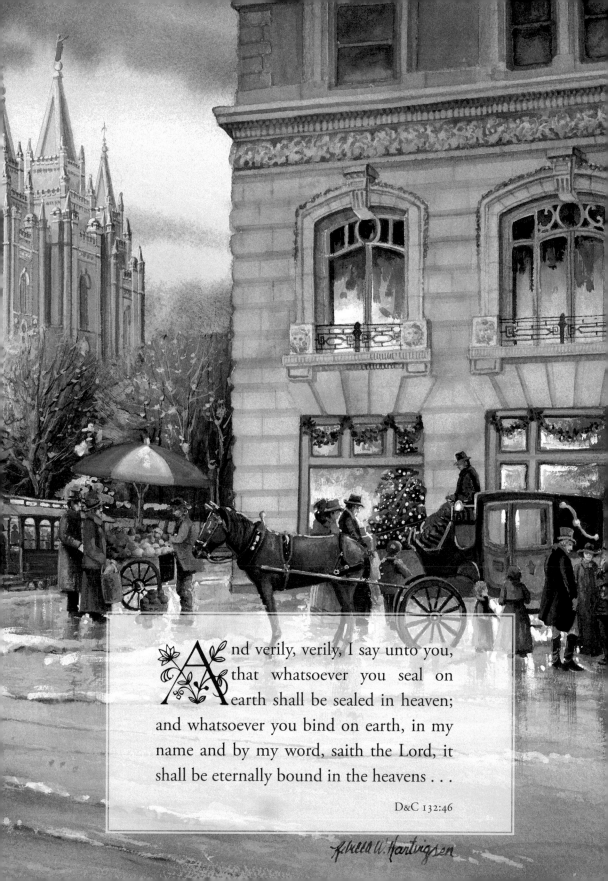

And verily, verily, I say unto you, that whatsoever you seal on earth shall be sealed in heaven; and whatsoever you bind on earth, in my name and by my word, saith the Lord, it shall be eternally bound in the heavens . . .

D&C 132:46

And again, verily I say unto you, I command you again to build a house to my name, even in this place, that you may prove yourselves unto me that ye are faithful in all things whatsoever I command you, that I may bless you, and crown you with honor, immortality, and eternal life.

D&C 124:55

Mesa Arizona

Logan Utah

et us truly be a temple-attending and a temple-loving people. . . . As we attend the temple, we learn more richly and deeply the purpose of life and the significance of the atoning sacrifice of our Lord Jesus Christ. Let us make the temple, with temple worship and temple covenants and temple marriage, our ultimate earthly goal and the supreme mortal experience.

HOWARD W. HUNTER, "A TEMPLE-MOTIVATED PEOPLE,"
ENSIGN, FEB. 1995, 5

Temples are places of personal revelation. When I have been weighed down by a problem or a difficulty, I have gone to the House of the Lord with a prayer in my heart for answers. These answers have come in clear and unmistakable ways.

EZRA TAFT BENSON, "WHAT I HOPE YOU WILL TEACH YOUR CHILDREN ABOUT THE TEMPLE" ENSIGN, AUG. 1985, 8

Bountiful Utah

Preston England

If you are geographically able, go to the temple on a regular basis. You will be better fathers and husbands, better wives and mothers. I know your lives are busy. I know that you have much to do. But I make you a promise that if you will go to the house of the Lord, you will be blessed; life will be better for you.

GORDON B. HINCKLEY, STAND A LITTLE TALLER
[SALT LAKE CITY: DESERET BOOK, 2001], 247

The temple is a house of prayer. . . . The temple is a house of instruction. . . . The temple is a house of revelation. . . . The temple is a house of commitment and sacrifice. . . . The temple is a house of solemn covenant. . . . The temple is a house of God where all of those declared worthy are extended the privilege of performing the sacred ordinances of the temple on behalf of their forebears. . . . There you will find peace; there you will come to know what security really is. There, in the house of the Lord, you can learn what you need to know to be truly free. There, tucked away from turmoil and strife, is the chance to be totally unselfish—a rarity in today's world.

Robert L. Simpson, "The House of the Lord,"
Ensign, Nov. 1980, 10

Idaho Falls Idaho

Dani Laura Wilson

Mount Timpanogos Utah

It is in the ordinances of the temple that we are placed under covenant to Him—it is there we become the covenant people. If we will accept the revelation concerning temple ordinance work, if we will enter into our covenants without reservation or apology, the Lord will protect us. We will receive inspiration sufficient for the challenges of life.

BOYD K. PACKER, THE HOLY TEMPLE
[SALT LAKE CITY: BOOKCRAFT, 1980], 265

For thou knowest that we have done this work through great tribulation; and out of our poverty we have given of our substance to build a house to thy name, that the Son of Man might have a place to manifest himself to his people.

D&C 109:5

Denver Colorado

Salt Lake City

And it shall come to pass in the last days, when the mountain of the Lord's house shall be established in the top of the mountains, and shall be exalted above the hills, and all nations shall flow unto it.

2 NEPHI 12:2

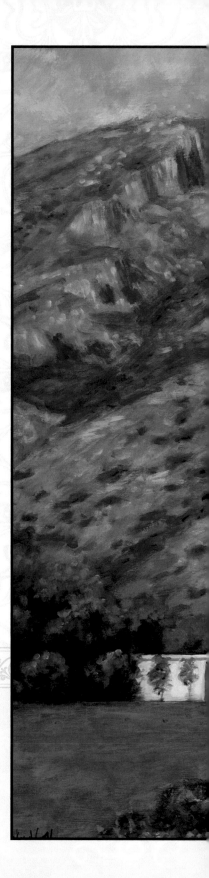

A Temple is more than chapel or church, more than synagogue or cathedral; it is a structure erected as the House of the Lord, sacred to the closest communion between the Lord Himself and the Holy Priesthood, and devoted to the highest and most sacred ordinances characteristic of the age or dispensation to which the particular Temple belongs. Moreover, to be indeed a holy Temple—accepted of God, and by Him acknowledged as His House—the offering must have been called for, and both gift and giver must be worthy.

JAMES E. TALMAGE, THE HOUSE OF THE LORD [SALT LAKE CITY: DESERET BOOK, 1968], 13–14

Provo Utah

Washington D.C.

rganize yourselves; prepare every needful thing; and establish a house, even a house of prayer, a house of fasting, a house of faith, a house of learning, a house of glory, a house of order, a house of God.

D&C 88:119

Laie Hawaii

Everything that occurs in the temple is uplifting and ennobling. It speaks of life here and life beyond the grave. It speaks of the importance of the individual as a child of God. It speaks of the importance of the family and the eternity of the marriage relationship.

GORDON B. HINCKLEY, STAND A LITTLE TALLER [SALT LAKE CITY: DESERET BOOK, 2001], 373

Newport Beach California

We build temples for the express purpose of having a holy place into which the worthy may go to perform ordinances calculated to bind together the living and the dead. Personally I should not like to contemplate the hereafter without my wife and my children, my parents and their parents, my brothers and sisters. I should not like to contemplate an existence, especially one that is going to continue forever, if I could not enjoy that existence with those whom I love. And so we build temples in the name of the Lord.

HUGH B. BROWN, THE ABUNDANT LIFE
[SALT LAKE CITY: BOOKCRAFT, 1965], 132

I promise you that, with increased attendance in the temples of our God, you shall receive increased personal revelation to bless your life as you bless those who have died.

Ezra Taft Benson, "The Book of Mormon and the Doctrine and Covenants," Ensign, May 1987, 85

Cardston Alberta

Vernal Utah

Let us, therefore, as a church and a people, and as Latter-day Saints, offer unto the Lord an offering in righteousness; and let us present in his holy temple, when it is finished, a book containing the records of our dead, which shall be worthy of all acceptation.

D&C 128:24

et me give you a definition in brief. Your endowment is, to receive all those ordinances in the house of the Lord, which are necessary for you, after you have departed this life, to enable you to walk back to the presence of the Father, passing the angels who stand as sentinels, being enabled to give them the key words, the signs and tokens, pertaining to the holy Priesthood, and gain your eternal exaltation in spite of earth and hell."

BRIGHAM YOUNG, DISCOURSES OF BRIGHAM YOUNG, SEL. JOHN A. WIDTSOE [SALT LAKE CITY: DESERET BOOK, 1954], 416

Logan Utah

Idaho Falls Idaho

And inasmuch as my people build a house unto me in the name of the Lord, and do not suffer any unclean thing to come into it, that it be not defiled, my glory shall rest upon it; Yea, and my presence shall be there, for I will come into it, and all the pure in heart that shall come into it shall see God.

D&C 97:15–16

One thing have I desired of the Lord, that will I seek after; that I may dwell in the house of the Lord all the days of my life, to behold the beauty of the Lord, and to enquire in his temple.

PSALMS 27:4

Salt Lake City

Rebecca W. Hartvigson

King Solomon's Temple

No jot, iota, or tittle of the temple rites is otherwise than uplifting and sanctifying. In every detail the endowment ceremony contributes to covenants of morality of life, consecration of person to high ideals, devotion to truth, patriotism to nation, and allegiance to God.

James E. Talmage, The House of the Lord [Salt Lake City: Deseret Book, 1968], 84

Through this work are the hearts of the fathers and those of the children turned toward each other. As the living children learn that without their ancestors they cannot attain a perfect status in the eternal world, their own faith will be strengthened and they will be willing to labor for the redemption and salvation of their dead. And the dead, learning through the preaching of the Gospel in their world, that they are dependent upon their descendants as vicarious saviors, will turn with loving faith and prayerful effort toward their children yet living.

JAMES E. TALMAGE, THE HOUSE OF THE LORD [SALT LAKE CITY: DESERET BOOK, 1968], 71

Nauvoo Illinois

Las Vegas Nevada

At the temple the dust of distraction seems to settle out, the fog and the haze seem to lift, and we can "see" things that we were not able to see before and find a way through our troubles that we had not previously known.

BOYD K. PACKER, "THE HOLY TEMPLE,"
ENSIGN, FEB. 1995, 36

But the Lord is in his holy temple: let all the earth keep silence before him.

HABAKKUK 2:20

Kirtland Ohio

Oakland California

Regular temple attendance is one of the simplest ways you can bless those who are waiting in the spirit world. If you live near a temple, partake of the opportunity to go *often* and *regularly*. If you live some distance from a temple, plan excursions so that you, too, might be uplifted and edified through this most satisfying and much-needed labor of love.

DAVID B. HAIGHT, "PERSONAL TEMPLE WORSHIP,"
ENSIGN, MAY 1993, 23

Where in 1847 nought but a wilderness of sagebrush and sunflowers stretched from the Wasatch barrier westward toward the shores of the great salt sea, now appears a stately city, even as was then foreseen in prophetic vision. On the site selected but four days after the advent of the pioneer band of "Mormon" colonizers, stands a massive structure, dedicated to the name of the Most High. It is at once an object of wonder and admiration to the visitor, and a subject of sanctifying joy and righteous pride to the people whose sacrifice and effort have given it being.

JAMES E. TALMAGE, THE HOUSE OF THE LORD [SALT LAKE CITY: DESERET BOOK, 1968], 113

Salt Lake City